W9-AOR-000

Meat-Eating Plants
Toothless Wonders

by Ellen Lawrence

Consultants:

Suzy Gazlay, MA
Recipient, Presidential Award for Excellence in Science Teaching

Dr. Robin Wall Kimmerer
Professor of Environmental and Forest Biology
SUNY College of Environmental Science and Forestry, Syracuse, New York

Kimberly Brenneman, PhD
National Institute for Early Education Research, Rutgers University
New Brunswick, New Jersey

BEARPORT
PUBLISHING

New York, New York

Credits

Cover, © Cathy Keifer/Shutterstock and © Daniel Gale/Shutterstock; 3, © Lazar Mihai-Bogdan/Shutterstock; 4, © Marvin Dembinsky/Photo Associates/Alamy; 5, © a9photo/Shutterstock and © Cathy Keifer/Shutterstock; 6, © Alessandro Zocc/Shutterstock; 7, © Chris Mattison/FLPA; 8B, © Cosmographics; 8–9, © Juniors/Superstock; 10, © Lazar Mihai-Bogdan/Shutterstock; 11, © Jaime Pharr/Shutterstock; 12, © Jan Van Arkel/FN/Minden/FLPA; 13, © Minden Pictures/Superstock; 13TR, © Cosmographics; 14T, © Peter Bulsing/FN/Minden/FLPA; 14B, © Cosmographics; 15, © Claude Nuridsany & Marie Perennou/Science Photo Library; 15TR, © blickwinkel/Alamy; 16B, © Cosmographics; 16R, © Photo Researchers/FLPA; 17, © Nature's Images/Science Photo Library; 18T, © Inga Spence/FLPA; 18B, © Cosmographics; 19L, © Noah Elhardt/Wikipedia Creative Commons; 19R, © EcoPrint/Shutterstock; 20–21, © Mike Stutz/Bearcats Photography; 21R, © Ch'ien Lee/Wikipedia Creative Commons; 22L, © Ruby Tuesday Books Ltd; 22TM, © Galushko Sergey/Shutterstock and © aquariagirl1970/Shutterstock; 22TR, © Ruby Tuesday Books Ltd; 22BM, © Danny Smythe/Shutterstock; 22BR, © picturepartners/Shutterstock; 23TL, © Jaime Pharr/Shutterstock; 23TC, © Lazar Mihai-Bogdan/Shutterstock; 23TR, © a9photo/Shutterstock and © Cathy Keifer/Shutterstock; 23BL, © Mike Stutz/Bearcats Photography; 23BC, © Minden Pictures/Superstock; 23BR, © Lazar Mihai-Bogdan/Shutterstock.

Publisher: Kenn Goin
Editorial Director: Adam Siegel
Creative Director: Spencer Brinker
Design: Elaine Wilkinson
Photo Researcher: Ruby Tuesday Books Ltd

Library of Congress Cataloging-in-Publication Data

Lawrence, Ellen, 1967–
  Meat-eating plants : toothless wonders / by Ellen Lawrence.
    p. cm. — (Plant-ology)
  Includes bibliographical references and index.
  ISBN 978-1-61772-589-0 (library binding) — ISBN 1-61772-589-7 (library binding)
  1. Carnivorous plants—Juvenile literature. I. Title.
  QK917.L395 2013
  575.9'9—dc23

                              2012014335

For more information, write to Bearport Publishing Company, Inc., 45 West 21st Street, Suite 3B, New York, New York 10010. Printed in the United States of America.

10 9 8 7 6 5 4 3 2 1

Contents

Trapped!

Venus flytrap leaf

A fly buzzing around a small plant lands on one of its red leaves.

The **insect** doesn't know it, but it has just made a big mistake.

It has landed on a plant called a Venus flytrap.

Suddenly, the leaf snaps shut!

The fly is now the plant's prisoner, and there is no escape.

> Why do you think the plant has trapped the fly?

Some of the leaves on a Venus flytrap have little hairs. These leaves act as a trap by snapping shut when something, such as an insect, touches the hairs.

Venus flytrap hair

Meat-Eating Plants

The Venus flytrap caught the fly to get the **nutrients** it needs to stay healthy.

Most plants don't get nutrients this way.

They take them in from the soil through their **roots**.

Some plants, however, grow in places where there are few nutrients in the soil.

These plants, such as the Venus flytrap, eat insects and spiders to get nutrients.

They are known as meat-eating plants.

How do you think a Venus flytrap gets the nutrients it needs from an animal's body?

grasshopper

Venus flytrap

a fly caught in a Venus flytrap leaf

One of the nutrients that meat-eating plants get from feeding on insects is nitrogen. Plants need nitrogen to help them grow—especially their leaves.

Good-bye, Fly!

Once a Venus flytrap catches a fly, the leafy trap squeezes shut.

Then the trap oozes juices that break down the soft parts of the fly's body.

The juices work like the liquids that break down food in a person's stomach.

As the fly becomes soft and soupy, the trap soaks up nutrients from the insect's body.

After about five days, the trap opens back up, and all that is left of the fly is its dry shell!

Venus flytraps live in the area shown in red. They grow in places called bogs where the ground is wet and soft.

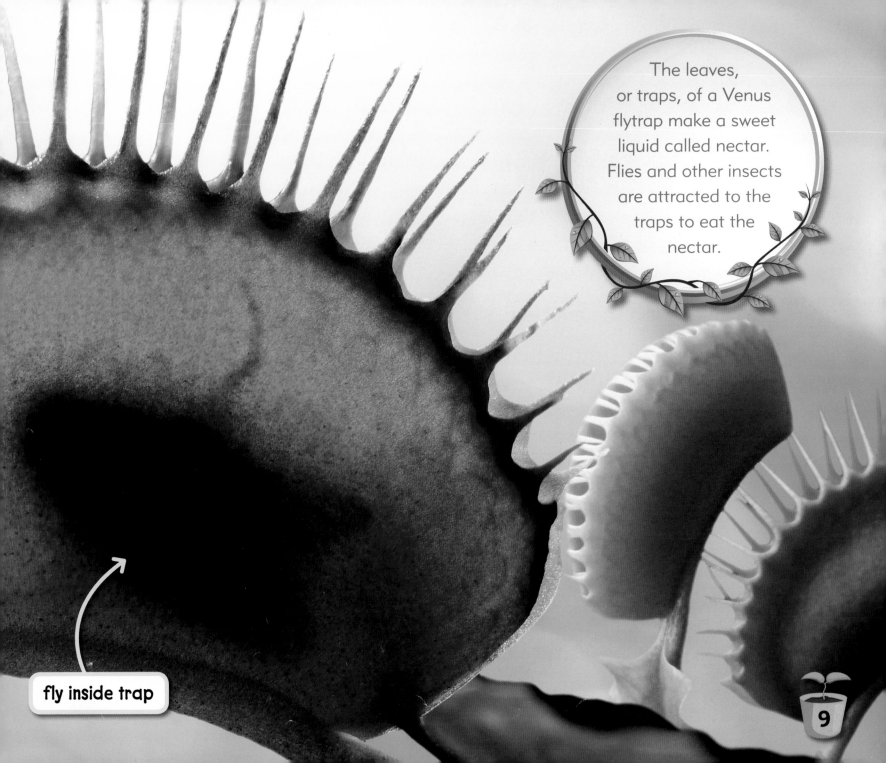

The leaves, or traps, of a Venus flytrap make a sweet liquid called nectar. Flies and other insects are attracted to the traps to eat the nectar.

fly inside trap

Food for Energy

To live and grow, meat-eating plants don't just need nutrients from insects.

They also need food for **energy**.

They make this food using water, a **gas** from the air called carbon dioxide, and sunlight.

They take in water from the soil through their roots.

The water moves up through the plants' stems and is stored in their leaves.

The leaves also collect carbon dioxide.

Then the leaves use sunlight to turn the water and carbon dioxide into food.

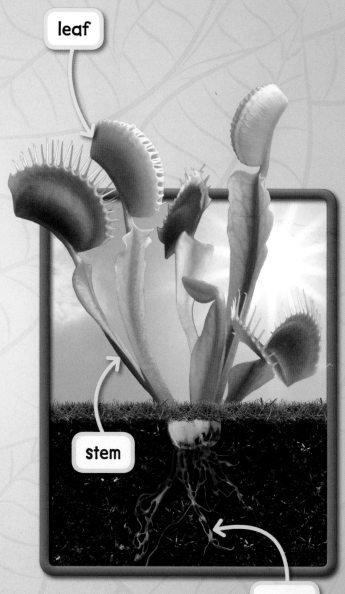

leaf

stem

roots

Venus flytrap plant

All plants use water, carbon dioxide, and sunlight to make the food they need. This process is called photosynthesis.

Some meat-eating plants do not have traps. They catch insects in other ways. Try to think of some ways they might do this.

A Sticky End

Sundews are meat-eating plants that use sweet-smelling, sticky glue to trap insects.

Their leaves are covered in tiny **stalks** that have a blob of glue on the tip.

When an insect lands on a sticky stalk, it gets stuck.

The leaf quickly curls around its victim and covers it with juices that make its body soft and soupy.

Then the leaf soaks up nutrients from the insect until only its shell is left.

a sundew leaf curling around a fly

Imagine that a friend of yours has never seen a sundew plant. How would you describe it?

sticky glue

stalk

sundew leaf

insect shell

Sundews live in the areas shown in red. They grow in wet places with spongy ground.

Arctic Ocean

North America

Europe

Asia

Atlantic Ocean

Africa

Pacific Ocean

South America

Indian Ocean

Australia

N

W   E

S

Southern Ocean

Antarctica

The sundew's glue smells sweet. Insects land on it because they think it is nectar that they can feed on.

Shiny Butterworts

A butterwort plant has leaves that look like they are covered in nectar or water.

When an insect lands on a leaf, however, it doesn't get a meal or a drink—it gets stuck!

The leaves look shiny because they are covered in sticky glue that traps tiny animals.

The leaves also make juices that turn insects into a soupy meal.

Then the plant can soak up the nutrients it needs.

butterwort plants

Butterworts live in the areas shown in red. They grow in places with wet, spongy ground.

a fly stuck
on a leaf

flies stuck on a
butterwort plant

hairs on a
butterwort

Tiny hairs
on a butterwort's
leaves make the
glue that traps insects.
Different hairs make the
juices that break up
the animal's
body.

15

A Watery End

Some meat-eating plants drown the animals they catch.

North American pitcher plants have a long pitcher, or tube, that holds watery liquid.

The top edge of the pitcher plant is slippery.

When an insect walks around the edge, it falls in and drowns.

The plant then soaks up the nutrients it needs from the dead insect's body.

North American pitcher plants

pitcher

North American pitcher plants live in the areas shown in red. They grow in places where the ground is very wet.

Pacific Ocean

North America

Atlantic Ocean

South America

N
W E
S

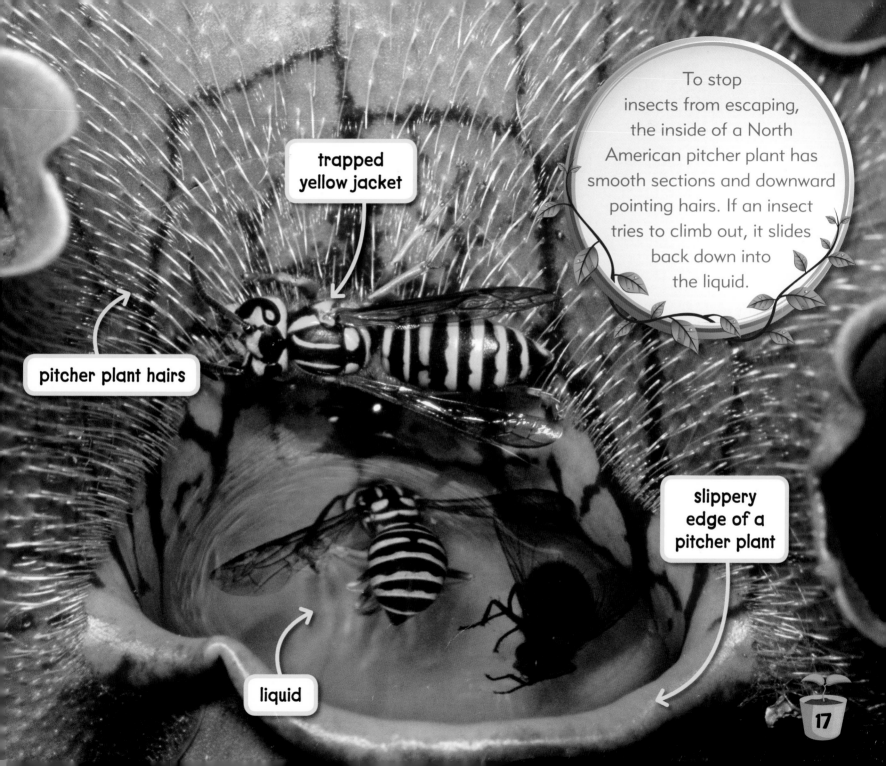

trapped
yellow jacket

To stop insects from escaping, the inside of a North American pitcher plant has smooth sections and downward pointing hairs. If an insect tries to climb out, it slides back down into the liquid.

pitcher plant hairs

slippery edge of a pitcher plant

liquid

17

Trapped by a Trick

California pitcher plants have a rounded, bubble-like part above their pitchers.

Insects crawl into the bubble to get to the plant's nectar.

When they try to find a way out, however, they get confused.

The bubble has many see-through patches that look like escape holes.

Insects crawl from patch to patch trying to escape until they are worn out.

Then they fall down into the pitcher's liquid and drown.

California pitcher plants

California pitcher plants live in the areas shown in red. They grow in places where the ground is wet and soft.

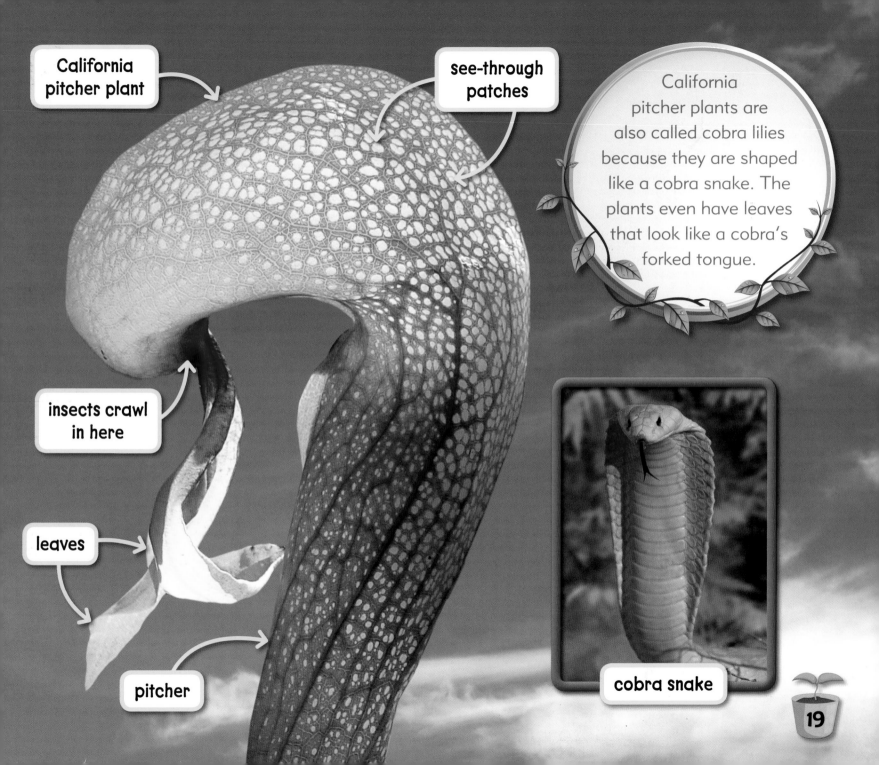

California pitcher plant

see-through patches

California pitcher plants are also called cobra lilies because they are shaped like a cobra snake. The plants even have leaves that look like a cobra's forked tongue.

insects crawl in here

leaves

pitcher

cobra snake

Insects Beware!

Meat-eating plants have many different ways to trap animals.

Some use sticky glue while others drown their meals.

Once an animal is trapped, the plant gets the nutrients it needs from the insect's body.

Meat-eating plants may look pretty and smell sweet, but if you're an insect, they are deadly killers!

> Which meat-eating plant did you like the best? Why?

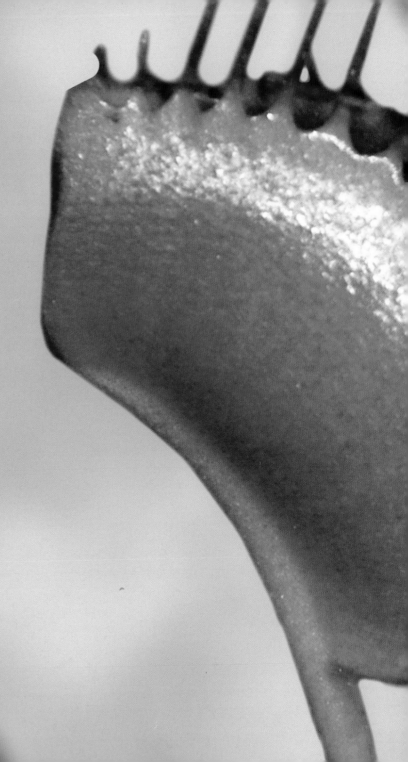

Sometimes rats and small lizards fall into large pitcher plants and drown. Then the plants eat these animals to get the nutrients they need.

a rat stuck in a pitcher plant

Science Lab

Be a Plant Scientist

Some plants get the nutrients they need by catching insects.

Most plants, however, get nutrients from the soil.

To find out what kind of soil is the best for growing bean seeds, plant some of the seeds in four different types of soil:

Soil 1	Soil 2	Soil 3	Soil 4

Soil from a garden or yard where plants are growing	Soil from an area where plants don't grow	Potting soil from a garden center	Sand or sandy soil

- *Which soil do you think the plants will grow best in? Why?*

- *Write down your prediction in a notebook.*

- *When the bean plants start to grow, which one grows fastest? Which one looks healthiest?*

- *Why do you think your prediction did or did not match what happened?*

Soil experiment step-by-step

Ask a grown-up to help you buy bean seeds and potting soil online or from a garden center.

❶ Collect the four types of soil. You will need enough of each soil to fill a small flowerpot or Styrofoam cup (with holes punched in the bottom).

❸ Place two bean seeds in each container, cover them with soil, and press down gently.

❷ Take four pots or Styrofoam cups and fill each one nearly to the top with one type of soil. Use a marker to label each pot or cup.

Soil 3

❹ Place the pots or cups in a sunny window. Water the seeds to keep the soil moist. Then keep watch to see what happens!

Science Words

energy (EN-ur-jee) the power needed by all living things to grow and stay alive

gas (GASS) matter that floats in air and is neither a liquid nor a solid; most gases, such as carbon dioxide, are invisible

insect (IN-sekt) a small animal that has six legs, two antennas, a hard covering called an exoskeleton, and three main body parts

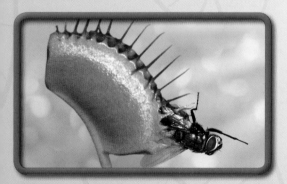

nutrients (NOO-tree-uhnts) substances needed by plants and animals to grow and stay healthy; most plants take in nutrients from the soil; meat-eating plants get them by eating animals

roots (ROOTS) underground parts of plants that take in nutrients and water from the soil; roots spread out in the soil to hold a plant in place

stalks (STAWKS) long, thin parts of a plant

Index

Read More

Batten, Mary. *Hungry Plants (Step into Reading).* New York: Random House (2004).

Fowler, Allan. *Plants that Eat Animals (Rookie Read-About Science).* New York: Children's Press (2001).

Platt, Richard. *Plants Bite Back! (Eyewitness Readers).* New York: DK Publishing (1999).

Learn More Online

To learn more about meat-eating plants, visit
www.bearportpublishing.com/Plant-ology

About the Author

Ellen Lawrence lives in the United Kingdom. Her favorite books to write are those about nature and animals. In fact, the first book Ellen bought for herself, when she was six years old, was the story of a gorilla named Patty Cake that was born in New York's Central Park Zoo.